Laughter Aloud

Laughter Aloud

(That's Life)

Mary-Christine Levett

Illustrations by Mark Bassett (autumn_19th@hotmail.com) and
Brenda Carrick (mclbjc@btopenworld.com)

Library of Congress Control Number:		2010914305
ISBN:	Hardcover	978-1-4535-8611-2
	Softcover	978-1-4535-8610-5
	Ebook	978-1-4535-8612-9

This book was printed in the United States of America.

To order additional copies of this book, contact:
Xlibris Corporation
0-800-644-6988
www.xlibrispublishing.co.uk
Orders@ Xlibrispublishing.co.uk
300938

Contents

Dedication

This book is for my family and friends
and anyone who loves laughter.

Acknowledgements

Kathy Wagner-Kimbrough for her help and encouragement always.

Mark and Aimee Bassett for their willingness to help with the illustrations and graphics.

Brenda Carrick for her help with the illustrations and graphics.

Carpe Diem
(Seize the day)

Come my friend, let's laugh and play,
Joy fill our hearts throughout the day,
So by tonight, all will say,
I'm glad I met you along the way.

Introduction

I have written this book of comic verses and stories over several years.

Each piece relates to life experiences at the time.

I think it is important to often look at the more humorous side of life.

The media largely concentrates on sadness and catastrophe; perhaps that is to help us realise that actually, most of the time, we are OK in our everyday lives.

My book is an attempt to redress the imbalance and encourage everyone to smile and laugh at some of the funny things that happen. If we can laugh at ourselves, then that gives other people permission to laugh too.

Garden Pests

Moles

My brother has a large garden, which he tends with great care and of which he is rightly proud. There are fruit trees, a vegetable patch, and beautiful flower borders. Imagine his distress at the invasion of a mole destroying his painstaking efforts and hard work.

Ode to a Mole

Is it a hump or is it a hole?
There's no need to worry 'tis only a mole,
Scraping and digging tunnelling away,
Searching for worms, to feed on today.

His smooth shiny coat, so sleek and so black,
Sharp claws for digging, at the front and the back.
He's well-kitted out to move through the earth.
He's blind as a bat and has been since birth.

No need for the light in this life underground.
His sharp sense of smell gets him easily round.
From tunnel to tunnel he goes on his way,
Upwards and downwards, working all day,
Until he comes out through a mound of fresh soil
To take in some air and rest from his toil.

M.B

The mole lifted his snout and with one final push
Shifted the soil neatly just under a bush.
He breathed in the air; it was fresh and so warm,
He was quite unaware that he might come to harm.
He sniffed again and was quite at his ease.
(Yesterday he'd come up surrounded by peas!)

But watch out, little mole, you'd better beware,
You've come up in a border of flowers so fair,
The gardener's not happy; he's fetching a trap
To catch you, alas, when you're taking a nap.
He rested there quietly upon a soft mound,
But felt a huge tremor come up through the ground.
The danger of heavy boots was close at hand,
Moving quickly, coming closer over the land,
To catch the mole, his work to spoil,
By filling the hole with castor oil.

Alas! Alack! This latest trick
Was guaranteed to make him sick.
So dig, little fellow, and don't be too slow.
You'll be safe in the darkness way down below.

The mole dug deep and deeper still,
Burrowing so fast with all of his skill,
To escape this last and final warning:
'Keep out of my garden, or you'll be dead by the morning!'

His spade-like claws sped through the dirt.
His snout and jaws on full alert.
His one last chance to get away
Was under the stream, to the field of hay.

Here only horses ran, and dogs were walked;
Where neighbours met and stopped and talked.

At last he stopped and dared to rise
To seek the air and paradise.
He listened long, and only heard
Distant sounds and harmless words.

The danger over in this new home,
Montgomery was free to roam.
He was safe at last and quite unhurt.
He had almost become a moleskin shirt!

An echoing voice blew through the air:
'You'd better stay put right over there.
That molehill you made
Has been thumped with a spade.
And with a great splat,
It's all been laid flat where you gently were sleeping
It's over—that's that!'

More Mole . . .

'Oh dear me, whatever next?'
Cried Grandma mole: 'I'm feeling vexed
At all this rain pouring down
Our burrow's flooding
We may all drown.'

'The water's rising, the tide is high.
The floods have come, our home's not dry
Our furs all wet, and the burrows damp.
Our claws are soft, and we've all got cramp.'

'There's nothing for it we'll have to go
To find another place that's dry below.
We may have to swim or at least to wade
Through all this mud to get some aid.'
'I hear there's shelter up the road.'
(Said Horace the friendly toad.)
Who came to see if they were all right
In the midst of the storm that rainy night.

So here we go, saved what we could
From our larder store, and bits of wood
Which may be useful in settling down
In another part of Wellington town.

Rabbits

For my poor brother, as if moles were not enough of a problem, a further pest in the shape of a rabbit then appeared and, of course, was able, at least for a short time, to enjoy fresh produce from the vegetable patch.

Rabbits in the Garden

The little furry bunnies are so cuddly and so cute,
We love to get a camera and do a photo shoot.
The only problem comes when growing up, these rabbits
Develop voracious appetites—one of their many habits.

Even little ones learn fast, eating everything in the garden,
Sitting on the lawn in sunshine without a 'beg your pardon'.
Gardener Mike is kind to them and sets a special trap.
Some fall for this and enter it—for them a great mishap.

He takes them out to a field in a far-off country lane,
Hoping that they won't find their way back to his plot again.
But so many more, it seems, replace the ones that have gone.
The munching in the garden just goes on and on and on!

Mike searches round the vegetable plot to see what he can do,
Then blocks the entrances with wire where they try to burrow thro'.
Somehow these little bunnies find alternative routes,
Still indiscriminately eating all the new plant shoots.

In desperation I said to Mike, 'The answer is a pie.
It's very sad, but these pesky rabbits really have to die.
Rabbit cooked upon the stove to make a very tasty stew.
It's the only way to stop 'em, that's what I would surely do!'

M.B

Pigeons

Sometimes it's birds that can present a problem. Pigeons, for example, are no respecter of persons when they need to go to the loo. I have often wondered why they have to open their bowels whilst in flight. It would be much less of a hazard, and cause of upset, especially to townsfolk, if they waited until they landed on the ground or a bush. I'm sure I am not the only person to have had this experience:

M.B

Pigeons

Splish! Splosh! Splat!
A pigeon shit upon my hat!
Now whatever shall I do,
To rid it of this messy poo?
How do people cope with that?
I'll leave my hat out in the rain,
To wash away this milky stain.
Oh no, it's shrinking!
And still it's stinking!
I'll never wear that hat again!

Mouse in the House

Thrice we have found mice in our house and garden.

The first mouse was extremely clever and made a hole where the telephone point comes into the house through the outside wall. It was able to scramble up the inside of the cavity wall and made a nest in the loft. It was only discovered because it was active at night and could be heard scampering above my room as I tried to sleep. At first I thought I was dreaming, but further investigation revealed a cosy little nest in the loft, made of paper, cardboard, and bits of cloth. A mammal trap was set with chocolate as bait. (Mice prefer this to cheese.) The mouse was caught and taken to the other side of the river and released, where we hoped it would stay in the fields. The hole in the wall was blocked up and all was well.

A few days later, while watering plants in the greenhouse, I heard a scratching noise from one of the flowerpots. Further careful and cautious investigation revealed two field mice leaping up and down. They had managed to jump in, and the pot was too high for them to jump out again. Had the same mouse returned with a mate? We will never know. The mammal trap was set with chocolate again, and this time the pair were taken to the top of the Downs before being set free.

Last week, I needed a nail to pin a notice to the gate. I kept them in neat little boxes in a drawer in the garage. As I opened the drawer, there was a quick movement, and a little brown mouse beat a hasty exit down the back of the unit. I haven't caught it yet, but the chocolate bait is ready . . .

Mouse in the House

Scampering quickly came the small mouse
Along by the wall and into the house
Through a hole in the door, where a dent in the floor,
Let him in quite hidden from view.

Sniffing the air with his whiskers atwitchin',
He savoured the smells coming out from the kitchen.
It was something to please, the smell of fresh cheese,
He scampered on without further ado.

Climbing up on a chair, he leapt onto the table.
He scratched at the cheese, until he was able
To reach out a paw, for a morsel to gnaw,
As the cat slept by the old chimney flue.

M.B

Munching and chewing, his brown eyes were glistening,
The cat opened one eye, and lay quietly listening.
The door opened a crack, as the cook she came back
To prepare a family dinner of stew.

Rubbing her eyes, she thought she was dreaming,
Gave a shriek and then began screaming.
Up leapt the cat, from his place on the mat,
And pounced at the mouse with a 'Meeoooo'.

The mouse was too quick, and was much too cunning,
He jumped from the table, and just kept on running
Without stopping to lick his whiskers now thick,
With the crumbs of the cheese that were blue.

My Family

When people first become acquainted with my family, they are often confused by the names. The reason is that several people share the same name, and lots of them begin with the letter 'M'.

A family 'Who's Who' is needed to sort out where everyone fits, and to help any listener to understand just which person is the topic of family conversations. It's a real gallimaufry of names for friends, and sometimes family too.

What's in a Name?

There's Dot and Mike, Mary, and Marg.
And then there's father and mother.
That makes three sisters when all is told,
And only one is a brother.

There's a lot of M's in our family,
Dot and Dad had to permanently utter.
'Michael, Margaret, Mary, and May.'
Amazing they both didn't stutter.
Matters got worse when they all married off;
Came in Michael, and Marg, and Martin.
Plus new sisters-in-law Marion, 'n' Mary
A muddle of M's then did begin.
So Dot's Mike, and Marg's Mart were renamed
With Mike's Marg and Marion's Mike also.
Marg's Mary, Mary L were adopted
And then it seemed all right. Oh!

But neighbours and friends were confused by these M's
Understanding was not any nearer
'Said you all choose nicknames without any fuss
For us it will become much clearer!'

More Confusion of a Different Nature

There are other things in life which can be very confusing; here's one of them: the names people give to toilets, or is it lavatories?

At Your Convenience

You have to go sometimes.
Well, don't you? When you're in the country or abroad.
Whether you're fully independent,
Or need assistance to pull the cord.
It's quite a natural function,
You can't get away from it.
But it's quite a tricky problem,
Knowing exactly where to sit
How can you ask directions?
If you don't know the right word?
Everywhere is different,
It's really quite absurd.
WC for water closet
Was the old-fashioned name.
But toilets have taken over,
That isn't quite the same.
his is fine in England,
But whatever do you do
When the Americans want the bathroom,
And they really mean the loo?
The Ozzies are the best though,
And really very funny,
Whether it's inside or in the outback,
They all request a dunny.

It seems a dictionary is needed
To solve this problem on ablution.
Perhaps a universal picture
Would be a natural solution!

Frustration

There are other more frustrating things in life. For me it's an absolute disaster if something happens to my computer.

A Virus

There's a virus in the system.
A virus I say.
I don't know where it came from,
But I wish it would go away.

It came across the Internet.
It just arrived today.
I must ring up the boffins,
To see what they have to say
To zap it, splat it, and clean it out some way.

There's a virus in the system.
A virus I say.
I don't know where it came from,
But I wish it would go away.

It's not a cold or 'flu' type,
Or a millennium bug,
Just a miserable, silent worm,
Causing much distress today.
Letters drop, attachments sent,
Words all come out queer,
There's no end to the chaos caused
It's enough to make one swear!
?*!!? ****!!?*****

There's a virus in the system.
A virus I say.

I don't know where it came from,
But I wish it would go away.

Drastic measures now we need,
To rid us of this pest.
An antidote is now required
Of Norton at its best,
To whine and gurgle, pip and beep,
Checking through the rest
Before it stops and squeaks.
It's found the cause so vile
You almost hear the virus squeal
As it's deleted from a file.

There's a virus in the system,
A virus I say,
I don't know where it came from,
But I wish it would go away.

I'd like to get my hands on
The small-minded little sod,
Who messes up the programmes,
And thinks he's playing God.
What a sad pathetic person,
Would want to cause such pain?
It's just as well once in there,
It can be taken out again.

There's a virus in the system.
A virus I say.
I don't know where it came from,
But at last it's gone away! Hooray!

More Problems with Computers

I had another mishap, when in a hurry one morning. The post arrived just as I was leaving. This is what happened!

Laptop Crunch

With bag in hand, and briefcase too,
Laptop secure, knowing what to do
And where to go, I unlocked the car
When at the gate the postman came,
Not early or late, on time the same.
Through the letter box the letters went,
Only one for me which had been sent.
So off to Horsham it's not far.
Start the engine, off I go.
Arrgh! There's a crunch from the wheels below.
As out of the gate I look back to see
What has happened? 'Oh dearie me!'
My lap bag and case lie flattened.
How on earth can that have happened?
They are not in the boot as I supposed
But lying squashed there in the road.

Doom and Gloom descend on me
'But all is not lost,' cries my friend B.
'The home insurance they will pay,
So contact them without delay.'

The drive's not broken, the story ends

Satisfactorily—thanks to friends.
The screen is shattered. The rest's intact,
All my work can be saved in fact,
Of which I am very glad indeed.
The lesson to learn I now must heed,
Put it all in the boot before you drive.
Then there's no disaster when you arrive.

Something to Think About

Sometimes there are things we really need to think about, and decide if they really are a good idea. Here's an example:

Genetic Fingerprinting

They'll take your DNA,
No matter what you say,
To be on the database,
Scientists say is really ace.

Your characteristics all on view,
Gives loads of info all about you,
The twisted double helix chain,
Never repeats its message again.
For you are unique; there's only one
Of you, when all is done.
Not even twins are quite the same,
There's no escape if you're to blame,

For if a crime you have committed,
As evidence it will be admitted,
'Guilty beyond reasonable doubt!'
Will be the jury's unanimous shout.
A sample from a swab of spit,
Has declared that you are it,
The person who has done the crime,
Was present at the scene this time.

Off to jail you will be sent,
Forever labelled as being bent,
If you are innocent, then you'll be freed,
A 'Not guilty' plea will be agreed.
So is it right or is it wrong?
A database to which we all belong?

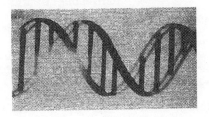

Farming in France

I enjoy travelling, both here in England and overseas. I have been fortunate in having both the opportunity and funds to do this.

Usually when I am having a holiday with a friend, and it is quite amazing to see what adventures come our way. I always keep a journal of the people we meet and the places we visit.

A few years ago, I had a friend who had a small farm in France, and during one visit we were able to watch sheep shearing. There were four sheep and an old ram called Bill. The sheep had young lambs; six in total. Our friends were almost self-sufficient, so the lambs usually ended up in the deep freeze. We had cleared the barn of sheep dung, the day before, and put fresh hay in the mangers.

The sheep had a large field in to munch grass and a large barn with fresh hay for shelter from the weather and for safety at night from predators.

Each sheep needed two men to catch and hold it. Old Bill, the ram, was first to be sheared, followed by the ewes. The fleeces were stacked on one side, and the sheep went bleating noisily back to the field. The lambs were quite upset because the ewes now smelt different, and they went searching in the barn, sniffing among the fleeces.

The sheep stayed out all day grazing. The barn was left open, and at dusk we took some sheep food in a bucket, and tried to persuade them to come into the barn by rattling the food bucket loudly. This was usually very effective, but that day the sheep were very reluctant to return to the barn. Perhaps, like elephants, they have good memories!

Eventually after dark, all the sheep went into the barn of *their own accord.*

Sheep

What a sight—these little lambs skipping in the field,
Unaware of future times, when the butchers axe he'll wield
Just once, their fate will be well and truly sealed!
Lamb chops for lunch that day.

The older sheep with shaggy coats graze on juicy grass,
Unaware that shearing time will quickly come to pass.
Woolly coats will quickly fall, and all will be exposed! Alas!
No dignity remains I'd say!

M.B

Old Bill the ram sulks miserably, among the hay and straw.
All pride is gone; the female sheep don't fancy him at all.
He turns his back on all concerned, and facing to the wall
Bleats piteously a 'Baay!'

Lambs cry out despairingly, searching for their Mum.
The sheep reply in chorus 'Maaaa!' And very quickly come
But looking, smelling different now, feeling rather numb
No longer want to play.

Back to the field they all rush out to take in the fresh air,
And baaing to each other, say: 'it really isn't fair'.
When night-time comes, what are we going to wear
To keep the cold away?'

As evening comes, the setting sun sends light across the trees.
The temperature drops suddenly, and it begins to freeze.
The barn doors open wide, and all the sheep can see,
It's fresh, soft, and juicy hay.

But they are stunned from shearing shock, and still are full of fear,
Despite the buckets rattling sound, falling on their ear.
The farmer is waiting patiently for them to enter here,
And shut them safe away.

Some of these sheep they are not dim, but are becoming brave
Venturing into the barn, their fleece less skins to save,
Drawn by the thought of food, and warmth, at last they begin to waive(r),
But they don't intend to stay!

When one takes fright, they all turn tail and rush outside again,
Stand by the door still looking in; the farmer tries in vain
With tasty food and drinking trough with water from the rain.
A most frustrating day!

M.B

'Leave them be' his wife declared: 'they'll come in when they're ready'.
She was right, later that night they came in sure and steady
All on their own, BAA!

Chickens

Seventeen chickens formed part of the family of animals on the farm in France. Each day I would let them out early, and scatter food for them, including any scraps left over from meals. The remains of the sweet corn harvest were also a favourite food for them.

After lunch loud clucking could be heard from the barn indicating that laying was in progress. After three thirty I would collect the eggs, and grade them according to size, ready for sale to the local people.

A cockerel was the proud head of this poultry family, and often I would be awakened by the persistent crowing announcing the dawn of a new day.

This experience served me well when a few years later the neighbours asked me to look after their chickens while they were away on holiday. No problem, here, apart from a broody hen who firmly sat on the nest in the hen house all day, and gathered all the eggs beneath her.

Donning gauntlets to prevented being pecked, I carefully removed her each day, much to her annoyance. Her response was to flap her wings in indignation and strut around the run, making a great deal of noise.

On both occasions the chickens needed to be shut in at night to protect them from local foxes on the prowl.

The following verses sum up the overall experience of looking after these feathered, farmyard friends.

M.B

Chickens

(Tune 'For all the saints who from their labours rest!' (*Sine nomine*)
For all the scraps left over every day
Fed to the chickens hoping they will lay
More eggs for breakfast clucking all the way
Cock, cock a doodle, cock a doodle do ooo.

One hen's gone broody, and stays on the nest
Sitting on straw to take a prolonged rest,
Hoping the eggs will hatch at her behest
Cock, cock a doodle, cock a doodle do ooo.

Put on the gauntlets. She has met her match.
Gather her up, so she can't bite or scratch
There is no chance these eggs are going to hatch.
Cock, cock a doodle, cock a doodle do ooo.

Now all the chickens are shut up so tight,
Safe in the hen house, hidden out of sight
From preying foxes, prowling in the night
Cock, cock a doodle, cock a doodle do ooo.

It's all been worth it, there are eggs galore.
Everyone is happy, who could ask for more?
What a great adventure; not at all a chore!
Cock, cock a doodle, cock a doodle do ooo.

Derbyshire

On another occasion, we were on holiday in the Peak District of Derbyshire. Each day we walked the dog on Grin Hill above where we were staying. At the top is Solomon's Tower, a folly with no particular use, built by a local farmer originally, and it marks the spot of an ancient burial ground. There are panoramic views at the top, and Kinder Scout, the highest point in the county can be seen in the distance. It's a very peaceful place.

A Walk in Derbyshire

Feel the breeze on your cheek and the wind through your hair,
As you climb to the top of the hill,
A stone tower stands tall and protects from the cold,
And the cows lie quiet and still.
Here the swallows can soar, swooping from dawn until dusk,
To catch their prey on the wing,
And grey rabbits abound, among moss-covered stones,
Where you can hear the redstarts sing.
You can see far and wide, from the east to the west,
A sweeping spectacular view,
Where close by at your feet, Parnassus so sweet,
And harebells of delicate blue.

Caverns in the Peak District

The caves in the Peak District are fun to explore, and they have a fascinating history. The semi-precious stone Blue John is mined from the caves.

The following two caves were our favourite:

Poole's Cavern has a legend that a robber by this name lived here in the fifteenth century and hoarded a silver cache.

Throughout the centuries, many visitors, including royalty, have come to the caves and been fascinated by them.

Writers and poets through the ages have all been impressed by their experiences in this cave and have written verses and prose of appreciation and wonder. I do not know if anyone has written in a light-hearted way, so here is my offering:

Poole's Cavern

Magic and mystery,
Steeped in history,
These were the caves, to which we came,
To a cavern, the locals called Poole,
After the man who sure was no fool.
He found silver, and so earned his fame.
A highwayman or robber?
Poole, who was this fellow?
Collecting silver as his swag,
For melting down in his fire,
Encouraging it with a bellow.
Fine silver coins—still they remain
Found in this earthy mire.

Limestone, our guide said
As upwards we were led,
In the darkness and danger and cold,
Then he put out his light,
This gave us a fright,
As we stood with nothing to hold.
Stalactites dripping down
In great drops on the ground,
Meet up with stalagmites from the floor,
Forming limestone pillars so thick,
You can't break with a stick,
And through which you can't possibly bore.

Peak Cavern or 'Devil's Arse' Cavern

This cave is reached by a path along a picturesque, narrow gorge. The entrance to the cave is huge, and is reputed to be the largest cave mouth in Britain.

Just inside there used to be a rope-making industry, and there is a demonstration of how this was done over the centuries.

The remaining caverns are reached by crouching along the side of the cave under the low ceiling. This was no problem for me, but for a tall person this would be quite difficult. In one place, the dripping stalactites formed a mound below. This was described as a poached egg, and we could see the likeness. In another cave the stalactites had formed a large structure, which was aptly named 'the flitch of bacon'.

One of the caverns has amazing acoustics, and it is lit by fibre optic lighting to highlight the magnificence of it. The next adventure in the cave system was to descend over one hundred steps. At the bottom was a stream, and a boat with a tour guide took us along an underground waterway to an underground lake. This is known as the 'Devil's Cellar' where you can hear the source of the river Styx. The roar of the water at certain times of the year supposedly sounds like someone farting, and has resulted in the cavern's name 'The Devil's Arse'.

This story was narrated by the guide, much to the amusement of the children in the group.

Peak Cavern or 'Devil's Arse' Cavern

Through little backstreets,
Along by the stream,
Pass the star white houses,
Idyllic, like a dream.
High cliffs sheer ascending,
Of grey and orange hue,
Surrounded by the woodland,
You do not have a clue,
That just around the corner,
Gaping large and wide,
The entrance hole to hell itself,
Gaping deep, and wide.
But no devil do you find here,
Though there is an old folklore,
That when the water's rising,
He farts up through the floor.
'The devil's arse' it has been called,
And for that very reason,
Folks of long ago believed it
For many a moon and season.

New Year in Devon, England

One of my favourite places is Lee Abbey on the North Devon coast. It is a great place for a retreat from the hustle and bustle of life. Even mobile phones are difficult to use; the reception is poor because of the surrounding cliffs and the hills of Exmoor.

One evening, over the Bank Holiday the gas supply ran out due to faulty pipes. The staff were faced with the problem of providing an evening meal for nearly two hundred guests. Here's the outcome . . .

No Food at the Inn

The tables set; the bell's not rung.
It's after seven, and we've had fun.
We're hungry.
A delay we hear from anxious staff;
The gas is off; it is no laugh.
We're hungry.

'It's not our fault.' declared the team.
BPs to blame, so it would seem
We're hungry.
The pipes are blocked. They're all unclean.
The filters stuck; a hopeless scene
We're hungry

We've a crisis here; they cannot cook.
What shall we do? Where shall we look?
We're hungry.
'Give some to me,' cried Lorraine and Chris.
'And some to Sue; we'll handle this.'
They're hungry.

So chips and fish, no special diet,
Were heated up to avoid disquiet,
For the hungry.

There's not enough; send to the pub
For more supplies; they've got good grub
For the hungry.

So guests were seated, the tables laid;
Some were patient; some dismayed
And hungry.
'How could this happen?' Some declared.
'Lee Abbey community's unprepared!
We're hungry!'

'Let's pray!' cried one. 'Take away!' cried another.
'Let's call a fast,' said a saintly brother.
We're hungry.
Some guests said, 'Humph'; some 'Oh dear',
Many said, 'Bah!' and were filled with fear.
All were hungry.

At last it's here! A tasty dish,
For all to share, of chips and fish
For the hungry.
The guests tuck in; all were well fed.
The crisis over; it's time for bed,
For the hungry.

Lessons were learned; but everyone wishes
We could return to the time of loaves and fishes,
To feed the hungry.

So finally, alack alas,
We must conclude God's not on gas
To feed the hungry.

The best fish and chips I have ever tasted!

Scotland

This was my first visit to Scotland. We flew from Gatwick to Inverness and then hired a car to drive to Skye, our first port of call. It was a truly enjoyable week despite the sometimes inclement weather. This is our journey to Skye.

On the Way to Skye

To Inverness and back again.
It's really easy to go by plane,
And take a hired motor car
To drive through the mountains far
Away to Skye.

To travel along beside Loch Ness
Which goes for miles, I must confess
I did not realise this, and so much more—
Panoramic views, wild flowers on the mossy floor
On the way to Skye.

Is the map needed? I don't know.
My driving companion knows where to go,
But checks on the mobile with daughter Sue
To ask if she knows what to do
On the way to Skye.

A hundred miles, we're nearly there,
Going along on a wing, and a prayer.
B phones ahead: 'We won't be long'.
Ian says he'll put the kettle on
When we arrive at Skye.

Over the bridge at the roundabout,
We turn left and without a doubt
We have gone wrong, so turn around.
The hotel at the next exit can be found
As we arrive in Skye.

A bar, TV, lounge, and cosy fire
Are all weary travellers could desire.
A lavish menu—beef, venison, and fish
With black pudding in chicken—a tasty dish
We are well fed at Skye.

The room is warm as we unpack
But a shout from the bathroom, 'Alas! Alack!'
'The water's hot,' cries B in pain.
'So add cold and try again!'
As we settle in at Skye.

Ian and Carol, we warmly greet.
They really are a pleasure to meet.
The room we have has three beds!
I just need one to lay my head
And fall asleep in Skye.

Kenya

We had many adventures in Kenya while on safari for two weeks. Of course, we saw many animals and learned a lot about them and their way of life.

One of the most surprising things was the way hippopotami roamed the grounds at night around the lodges where we were sleeping.

Here is the proof that they were close by!

Night Visitors

To greet the day, I threw open the door,
Only to discover on the forest floor,
A dump of the most amazing size,
Just six feet away, to my surprise
Hippos had grazed there in the night,
Leaving their trademark, what a fright!
A huge footprint was also found,
Clearly imprinted on the ground,
To show where this gigantic beast
Had stopped to munch his midnight feast,
So close to where I lay fast asleep.
This thought alone made my skin creep.
The Maasai guard patrols the land,
A wooden club held in his hand,
So no need to tremble or to fear.
When this monster of the night draws near,
I know it's a herbivore of course,
Only a huge aquatic horse.

Lions

There were lots of lions in Kenya. We saw a solitary male feasting on a zebra which he had killed. More often, the lions were in groups. The most memorable occasion was seeing a family pride resting by the water. We were at the top of a rise overlooking the waterhole and had an excellent view from this vantage point. The safari guide, however, warned us that the male lion was keeping a close eye on us from behind the minibus. He was completely camouflaged by the dried grass.

Hungry Lions

The lions are coming, prowling through the grass,
Don't move an inch,
Or even flinch,
But watch them quietly pass;
For if you shout or jump about
It will be the end of you, alas!

M.B

Big Spotted Cats

During our travels across the game reserves, we saw both cheetahs and leopards. The latter are quite rare and it is quite easy to confuse the two big cats. Often the spotted appearance may vary, but the key identifying feature is the black eye marking prominent in the cheetah. These are absent in leopards. The leopards also climb trees, but cheetahs are less likely to be found in trees, existing in the open savannah and grasslands.

Big Spotted Cats

Cheetahs and leopards are found where it's hot;
Both are black and white and covered in spots.
But to see the difference you must be wise
And get close enough to look at their eyes.

Is it a cheetah asleep on the tree?
If you look closely, you'll be able to see
Black marks on his face and you can decide
If it is one, then it can't be denied.

On closer inspection you find and recall,
It's a leopard indeed with no tear marks at all.
The fast-running cheetah stays close to the ground
To catch unwary prey who may be grazing around.

For leopards have no markings to show.
The difference between them you always will know.
You can identify this beautiful cat
One of the big five, you can be certain of that.

Australia

Visiting Australia was such an adventure, filled with unexpected events and surprises.

We (my friend BJ and I) arrived in Sydney in the early hours of the morning, exhausted from the long flight and feeling rather jaded at the edges. Our hotel room was comfortable enough, and to refresh ourselves before turning in for the rest of the night, we decided to take a dip in the rooftop swimming pool.

This was indeed an enjoyable experience until . . .

Cockroaches

As I surfaced from the water, much to my surprise,
Little, scurrying creatures met my weary eyes.
Everywhere you looked, these armour-plated beasts
Were exploring the rooftop for a midnight feast.

M.B

I looked a little closer, and carefully did approach,
Only to discover each was a shiny brown cockroach.
Whatever are they doing here, on this rooftop high?
Are there other creatures lurking in those bushes nearby?

Snakes or alligators may be close at hand,
You never know what's out at night, in this foreign land.
So leaping from the water, increasingly alarmed,
I rushed back to the bedroom, before I could be harmed.

When morning came, I went back to the pool.
No crocodiles, snakes, or cockroaches, I really felt a fool.
It's amazing in the night-time what comes into your mind,
In your exhaustion, you can see creatures of every kind.

Aargh! I am not squeamish, you understand about creepy crawlies normally, but then I don't usually encounter them when in my swimming costume. At that hour of the night, I wondered what other creatures might be lurking in the surrounding area, or indeed in the water. This after all was the land of crocodiles and alligators, and who knows what kind of pets the locals might keep.

We made an immediate decision to return to the hotel room with our imaginations working overtime about the possible nocturnal habits of Australian fauna. I slept well, perhaps surprisingly, and all seemed normal in the morning. We were able to laugh at our reaction from the previous night. We did not, however, venture near the pool to swim again, just in case . . .

The Crocodile Farm

What an exciting place! Here we found crocodiles and alligators in their natural environment. They looked almost harmless, lazing in the sun. They kept very still and didn't move; they could have been mistaken for logs because their skins are green, hard, and scaly.

Some, however, had their mouths wide open, displaying their huge teeth. That was a bit more daunting, especially when the keeper told us that their jaws were very powerful and strong enough to crush bone.

Here the farm produces meat and crocodile skins to export to the countries.

In the restaurant, crocodile meat was on the menu, and I did try it. It had hardly any taste and looked a bit like chicken, so I was unimpressed. It would need a very piquant sauce to accompany it to make it appetising.

We watched one keeper feeding a crocodile in a shallow pool. Lunch for this magnificent beast was a chicken carcase, at the end of a long rope.

At first, we couldn't see the crocodile, but as the keeper whirled the chicken carcase around at the water's edge, there was a sudden flurry of activity. The huge jaws of this crocodile grabbed the chicken with a very loud 'snap', and it was pulled quickly under the water. The crocodile had the chicken securely between its teeth and rolled over and over in the water. If it had been a person, he would have drowned for certain, before being eaten alive. I found this quite scary, and it sent shivers down my spine.

I noticed that the keeper made sure he knew the position of the crocodile at all times during the display. He also always had a clear escape route to the gate so that the wily crocodile couldn't trap him in the enclosure. I thought it very wise for the keeper to know the behaviour of the animals and to respect them.

As we continued round the park, we came across two people crouching by the fence to get a close-up of an alligator. It was irresistible not to clap my hands once suddenly behind them. Yoicks! They jumped back in fright, as though the alligator itself had lunged at them. It, however, had not moved and continued to sleep peacefully in the sun. Fortunately, they laughed with us at such a trick.

Ode to the Mighty Crocodile

Did you ever see a crocodile up close and count his teeth
Or watch him grab unwary prey, and haul it underneath
The water, tightly held, where the victim's fate is sealed.
Did you ever see a crocodile hiding in the murk,
Pretending to be half-asleep, when with a sudden jerk—
His jaws gape wide, and with a 'snap', he's snatched another meal?
A mighty beast with evil eye, strong legs, and swishing tail.
Fifteen feet if he's an inch of armour-plated mail!

M.B

Large Flightless Birds

We had seen ostriches in the countryside, as we travelled through Australia, and there were frequent road signs warning of their existence, and habit to wander in the road. They are strange birds indeed with their long legs, and feathered, barrel-shaped body. I find their colour dull; both the grey/fawn of the female ostrich and the black body of the male. They behave by running, seemingly, without reason, and pecking in the ground for seeds and grass with their large beaks. They are reputed to bury their heads, but I didn't see this happen.

At home, we have an ostrich egg, which we bought from a craft shop. It is a very large, hard egg, nearly 15 cm in diameter, and painted on the outside with an elephant design.

As we continued on our way around the park, we came next to the cassowary pens. These large birds are related to ostriches, but slightly smaller than them and certainly more brightly coloured with their blue heads and red necks.

Cassowaries are renowned for their fierceness, and as we approached the fence to take a closer look, one of them advanced with a typical aggressive neck jerking stance.

It then turned and it kicked the fence with both feet displaying the three strong toes on each foot.

It was quite daunting. The keeper explained how to raise your hand in the shape of the cassowary's head and move it in the same jerky way. On seeing this, the cassowary became less aggressive because it thinks a taller, stronger bird has appeared and is threatening it.

I wondered how it would react if you mimicked its kicking action; I didn't try.

On the Cassowary

A strange bird by all accounts, is all that I can say.
Neither emu nor ostrich she; but related in some way.
Pretty birds to some degree, with feathers red and blue.
Sharp beaks, long legs, and triad feet, I've seen them this is true.
Approach with care I've heard it said, and hold your hand up high.
Jerk and dart, and dart again, if you would pass her by.
For safety's sake take my advice. Don't offer any food.
She'll spit and kick, and kick and spit, if she is in the mood.

Kangaroos

We were in Australia for four weeks, and we travelled from the north of the country to the south. In all that time, we did not see a kangaroo in the wild. There were many roadside signs warning that they were in the area. Everyone we met assured us that there plenty about, but they must have seen us coming and hidden in the bush. Beth, the friend with whom were staying, drove us out into the bush to look for them. All we saw was a flattened piece of grass, where we assured that one had slept the previous night.

We did see them in the nature reserve at close quarters, so we had to come to the following conclusion:

M.B

Lost Kangaroos

They say they're everywhere in Australia, near towns and in the outback,
Clearly seen on golf courses, and along every country rough track.
At dusk alongside every road where the signs are written plain,
And at noontide in the sunshine, asleep in grassy lush terrain
I've searched on foot throughout the bush, passing through dense forest green,
And driven slowly up the track, but there's not one to be seen.
From north to south I've searched for them, and followed tracks galore
On foot, by car and aeroplane, I've scoured the land right o'er.
The Ozzies are convincing which adds to my confusion,
But having thought about it all, I come to one conclusion:

There Are No Wild Kangaroos in Australia!

Koala Bears

While in Australia, we had booked a trip to the Blue Mountains to see the eucalyptus trees, and hopefully koala bears in their natural habitat. Unfortunately, that day there was a controlled bush burning programme in progress, and we were unable to enter the national park. We could see the blue haze in the distance, from the eucalyptus trees that give them their name, and had good views across part of the forest and stony outcrops. We looked up many eucalyptus trees during our holiday, but there were no signs of koalas. We saw them at close quarters, later, in one of the wildlife centres.

Up a Gum Tree

Blue haze in the mountains,
Fragrance in the bush,
Peeling bark on white trunks,
Waving fronds so lush . . .
But where are the koalas
Where are these little bears?
Munching on the new shoots
Which everyone declares
Is what they like to feed on
As their favoured feasts,
But I can't seem to find 'em,
These furry little beasts.
My eyes are tired from staring
Up many a grey-green tree
I've a crick in my neck.
Oh, what the heck!
I'll think I'll let 'em be

M.B

Duckbilled Platypus

The disappointment of not seeing kangaroos and koala bears in the wild was partially offset by the sighting of duckbilled platypus swimming in a backwater.

M.B

Duckbilled Platypus

There it was suddenly swimming in the stream.
A duckbilled platypus; I thought it was a dream.
But there it was in real-life paddling through the water,
Diving here, and diving there; content in every quarter.
This amazing little creature, behaving quite naturally,
An unexpected encounter, we were privileged to see.

Australian Magpies

Down in the south near Melbourne there was an encounter of a different kind. Australian magpies woke us each day with their characteristic song: doodle, oodle, oodle, oooo.

Doodle, Ooodle, Oodle, Oooo

To wake you from your dreams, so early in the morning,
Comes the sound of magpies, suddenly without warning.
Doodle, ooodle, oodle oooo.

On and on he's singing in the garden trees outside.
No further rest is possible; it's there he will abide.
Doodle, ooodle, oodle oooo.

Now I don't mind a cockerel that crows at early dawn,
But the Australian magpie is one I surely scorn.
Doodle, ooodle, oodle oooo.

I'll just have to put up with it, this mournful morning sound
I've tried throwing things at it; they only hit the ground.
Doodle, ooodle, oodle oooo.

So out of bed, to rise 'n' shine, and start another day
Let out the cat to chase after it. Then it will go away
Doodle, ooodle, oodle ooooooooooooooooooo.

M.B

Day Out in Old Sydney Town (An Extract from My Journal.)

Well, here I am in Oz—yes, Oz, Australia.

It's autumn, pleasantly cool with hazy sunshine and the day's adventure awaits as Zillah and I drive to Old Sydney Town.

I've arrived here in New South Wales having travelled north to Cairns from Sydney having experienced rainforests, the Great Barrier Reef, and a taste of aboriginal culture. Wildlife, inside and outside, game reserves have added to this exciting trip, including crocodiles and cassowaries and kangaroos and koalas, not forgetting squawking screeching cockatoos, and tuneful magpies piping their song at dawn as the sun rises over the blue hazy mountains.

Now a half hour trip from Newcastle brings us to the entrance of Old Sydney Town, where the first attraction is a giant-sized model koala, complete with 'Ozzie' outfit including bush hat with corks. We take a photograph just for the record and future reflections, then enter the time tunnel and come to the costume booth. Here, two solemn gentlemen in eighteenth-century dress are posing for a picture with their spouses, who are also dressed in the spectacular finery of the times.

They are desperately trying not to laugh as the photographer disappears under a cloth, covering a camera set on an old-fashioned tripod. A flash indicates that the snapshot has been taken.

The photographer emerges from under the black cloth, and disappears into the back of the booth. Five minutes later, and the result is an authentic picture in sepia portraying the foursome in their finery.

We decided that this activity was worth doing, and giggling like schoolgirls, we dressed up as two 'floosies' of the times as shown in the pictures. The best way to describe the fun we had has been described in the following light-hearted verses.

All Dressed Up and Nowhere to Go!

Hey! Look at you!
Dressed up in blue
With a feather in your hat!
With low cut neck!
Oh, where the heck
D'ya get a diamond like that!?
With boobs thrust out
Beyond a doubt
Ye're a hussy that's a fact!
See your delight
In fishnet tights
Just see the way ye're sat

Half empty gin!
It is a sin!
Turnin' to drink that's flat!
See all that red!
From toe to head;
It's clear what game you're at!

Where's the fun
In cards and gun?
There's a bloodstain on the mat!
Y'don't know half!
What a laugh!
Behaving like a prat!

REWARD

here's a good likeness, 'cept it ain't as ugly as the real thing.

Then clutching our sepia 'wanted' poster and coloured photograph, we continued mirthfully on our way through the town streets.

We next met a rather pompous looking beadle strutting along in knee breeches and buckled shoes, long jacket and black hat, the latter seemed to be worn by all the men in various states of tattiness and often very battered. This gentleman, however, was smartly dressed, and I asked Zillah to take a photograph. I wanted to be in the picture too, so approached the portly fellow and grabbing his arm said, 'Excuse me, sir, I need some support here.'

He replied, without twitching a muscle of his podgy face,

'Madam, with a body like yours I would need support too!'

What an insult! What affrontation!

Zillah dissolved into helpless laughter at his words, and although taken aback at the rapid insulting retort, the humour of the situation prevailed, and the photograph was successfully taken.

We wandered through the streets until we came to the local inn 'The Black Dog', where I felt homesick momentarily as I thought of my own two black Labradors back in Sussex and wondered what everyone there was doing today and wished that they could be part of this great adventure.

We ordered beer and sandwiches and sat outside in the courtyard awaiting the next spectacle of army recruitment. Dressed in the uniform of the day, a sergeant and three soldiers appeared, parading up and down, going through drills and exercises, to impress the crowd.

The sergeant called for young male 'volunteers' and moved amongst the customers searching out 'willing' lads who fitted the bill.

Several young men were game for a laugh, and entered into the recruitment programme with gusto. They were put through their paces for mental and physical suitability, maintaining cheerful cheeky banter with the soldiers. Only one of the volunteers was finally selected; the rest spurned for their lack of physical agility and mental prowess.

We followed the soldiers down to the parade ground for the firing of cannon balls from real canons. The sergeant shouted the orders and suggested we cover our ears to prevent becoming permanently deaf from the noise. He suggested that should anyone want to take pictures, that another person cover *their* ears while this was done. The village idiot was on hand to provide this service for a small fee.

The canon was duly fired and was indeed loud. I had not realised that these leaden balls would travel for over a mile and was intrigued by the preparation of the shot.

We enjoyed this spectacle immensely before continuing on our way to the bottom of the town, admiring the costumes of the shopkeepers, and lay out of the tiny shops with their dark interiors. Eventually, we came to an old farm track, where an ancient covered wagon, pulled by oxen, was waiting for the unwary visitors and tourists. The drover was dressed in a simple smock, gaiters made of sacking tied with string, and a battered hat. He invited us to join him; his tone was jovial and light, and we happily climbed into the cart.

The cart held a dozen people in all, and there were eight oxen in the team. The drover explained that the front two were the leaders guiding the cart; the two at the back 'to steady 'em' and the middle four were 'fer pullin'

Off we went with the cart, immediately lurching wildly from side to side over the rough ground. The drover flicked his long whip lightly over the steers. All 'passengers' were forced to cling on tightly to each other, or to the edge of the wagon. We inched slowly forward, progressing up an incline, and round a long curve which only had the result of intensifying the sway of the cart, and increasing the terror of its occupants.

The oxen stopped suddenly halfway up the slope in the muddiest part imaginable. The drover said, 'This is the place for those to get off wot's had enough.' Unsurprisingly no one took up his offer, and we continued erratically on our way, circumventing a knoll before arriving back at the starting point.

Returning to the centre of the town, we both felt sorry for the oxen confined to a life of walking round the same boring circuit, day after day for the benefit of the tourist industry, and vowed not to ride on the wagon next time.

SMOKERS WILL BE
SEVERELY BEATEN
ABOUT THE
HEAD AND BODY

At the post office we stopped to buy postcards and some souvenirs below a large sign which proclaimed that:

We debated whether this was for the twenty-first or eighteenth century and decided it was appropriate for both.

Exhausted but happy we returned home; we had had a most enjoyable day.

California

I have visited the United States several times and have always found Americans very hospitable, friendly, and helpful.

On one occasion, I was attending a Louise Hay conference in San Diego, and there were people there from many countries, including from states across America. The visit was made even more enjoyable by visits to San Diego zoo and to the homes of the team members in the foothills outside the city.

Visit to Mission Beach San Diego

Mission Beach

Oh what a mess, what a mess, what a mess from the pelicans on the rock,
And the stink of the seals on the shore,
The pigeons squabbling noisily on the strand above,
Who could ask for more?

The pelicans with beaks so large,
And the seals asleep on the sand,
The pigeons with bright feathers preened,
Eating greedily out of your hand.

The seagulls screeching loudly overhead,
Where the ships sail into the docks,
I stand and watch the rollers out in the bay,
Crashing spray against the rocks.

People

People are fascinating just because of who they are and the things they do. For example, my friendly neighbour Nelson used to walk our dogs every day. This is an appreciation written for his eightieth birthday. Sadly he has passed on, and we miss him very much.

Ode to Nelson

He's a really nice sort of chap
In his red baseball cap
Which he wears on his head as he will
And when you hear humming
You know he is coming
Back from his walk on the hill.

It isn't a rumour
His dry sense of humour
Can amuse you with many a ditty
He's told many jokes
To all sorts of folks
And can be remarkably witty
But Audrey's not sure
She's heard them before
And sighs and says
What a pity!
He comes to the gate,
And rarely is late,
To collect both Muffin and Bramble.
They know he's a treasure,
Wag their tails in great pleasure,
They're off to fields for a ramble

When the weather is wet,
He never does fret,
But off to his shed goes hiking,
Where wielding a spanner,
In a professional manner,
He fixes your wheels to go biking.

Now armed with a strimmer,
He keeps himself slimmer,
And out on the bank goes a mowing.
It's never a bovver,
To keep using his 'Hover'
On the bank where the grass keeps on growing.

When it's time to go out,
He's off with a shout:
'You get on with your darning.
I'm off to see Michael,
Down the lane on my cycle
For a jar and a long night of yarning.'

So to Nelson we say:
Happy Birthday!
Have a drink on us today matey
We're so proud of you
And the things that you do.
Not bad for a bloke just turned eighty!

Exam Marking

Another friend of mine marks examination papers each year. There are fixed deadlines and the pressure for a few weeks is enormous as the workload is tackled. Not only is there the task of marking scripts, but also the packaging and posting of scripts to be returned to the examination board.

Here's a light heart look at the process . . .

Ode to Exam Markers

> She woke with a sneeze,
> And was at once at ease
> With the work she had to do.
>
> With a yawn and a stretch,
> She was ready to fetch
> Her pen, and begin anew.
>
> With a hot cup of coffee,
> A mint, and a toffee,
> She knew she would soon get through.
>
> So with pen poised at the ready,
> She marked true and steady,
> Until the date they all were due.
>
> Phew!

Misspent Youth

Sometimes people, when enjoying themselves, let situations get out of hand. This can happen especially when they have drunk too much alcohol.

Here is an example of what happened to one famous teenager after a night out, celebrating the end of GCSE. The incident was widely reported by the media.

The Dangers of Misspent Youth

'It isn't fair!' cried Euan Blair.
'I've been arrested in the square.
Mr Plod while on his beat,
Found me lying in the street.
I couldn't stand up on my feet.

Daddy is at Number 10.
Don't know when he'll be out again
I only see him 'now and then'.
Mummy is also still away,
With grandma on a holiday.
'I don't know what to do or say.'

'We must stop this little antic,'
Said his father, 'I'm quite frantic',
(Trying not to sound pedantic.)
'Down to the station you're in trouble.'
He was marched off at the double,
To try and mend this mess and muddle.
'Why d'ya do it tell us why?'
Was the angry parents' cry.
'What can we do? Oh my! Oh my!'
'It only was a little drink.

I didn't really stop to think,'
Said Euan, turning rather pink.
This added to his father's rage.
'You're only sixteen, under age.
You should be locked up in a cage.'
'I know that, Dad.
I'm sorry that I made you sad,'
Replied the very contrite lad.
'But to the bank we now must go,
And get the £100 you owe,
For all that swaying to and fro.'
To the station he's been brought,
There's a lesson to be taught:
To stay sober is what he ought.

A little chat with Mr Plod,
Soon sorted out the little sod.
'It's over now', he said, 'thank God!'
Education! Education!
The panacea for the nation,
Preventing further devastation
Every child in every school,
Must now learn the golden rule,
'Alcohol makes you a fool.'

Justice was surely done on this occasion, but I wonder about the second incident described in the following verses. This time the young man in question was on holiday, staying at a hotel in Italy, and messing about with his friends when using the lifts late at night.

More Misspent Youth

What a noise,
Boys will be boys,
And make a great commotion.
It's such a lark,
When after dark,
To keep the lifts in motion.

'Shhhhh! There's good chaps,
Prevent mishaps!'
The manager exclaimed,
'Now go to bed
Before too much is said,
And no one will be blamed.'
'What a mess,
It's in the press!'
Cried Cherie to dear Tony,
'It's headline news,
Refute these views, as Italian boloney.'

Number 10 played it down,
Euan Blair he is no clown.
The report came out on Monday.
That news came through, to me and you;
A 'U'-turn was made from Sunday.

This new decision, caused some derision,
But we must understand,
The weight of guilt, has made them wilt,
The press had the upper hand.

So do not drudge, or bear a grudge,
And let that be the end.
For little Theo, or is it Leo,
The public rift will mend.

Elders of Excellence

Older people can be great fun too and get up to as much mischief as young people. Like this for example:

My Walking Stick

'Hey, you there, Dick,
That's my walking stick,'
Cried Amy from her chair.
'What's your game?
There's your frame
Standing over there.'

'Caught you napping,'
Said Dick clapping
With a toothless grin,
'Toilets calling,
I'm scared of falling,
You're not going anywhere!'

Off he went,
With back all bent,
Aiming for the door,
He tripped and fell,
Amy rang the bell,
As Dick began to swear.

'Serves you right
To have a fright.
Pride comes before a fall.
You'll think twice
About being nice;
It's better after all.'

Health Checks

From time to time we all have problems with our health and need to seek help from the doctor, dentist, optician, and others.

I See (A Visit to the Optician)

'Open your eyes
As though in surprise,
I'll just put a little drop in.
Then with a puff
Of some air like stuff,'
My smile fell off my chin
'Oh me! Oh my!'
I said with a cry.
'I can't see a flippin' thing.'

'Watch my small light,
As I examine your sight,
I'll just have a look inside.
Which is lighter?
Is red or green brighter?
I need you to be my guide.
What can you see?
K, J, L, or P?'
'I can only read "A",' I replied.

'Glasses are needed,'
I sighed and conceded:
'I think I will have to agree'.
Choosing a frame
Was quite a new game.
But at last I can finally see!

Dentists

Visiting the dentist can be quite a daunting, even slightly scary experience. This is nothing compared to a visit to the hygienist as I discovered recently.

The Tooth Scraper (A Visit to the Hygienist)

'Hold your toothbrush at an angle,
This idea's a new fangle,
Add the toothpaste; just a bit,
Take care not to swallow it,
Complete the action; learn to spit.'

With pick and hoe to scrape the teeth,
And remove the debris underneath,
Keep very still; don't move your head
Grinding with a cement paste
She whizzed around with undue haste,
Until my gums, they freely bled.

'No worries,' quoth she unconcerned,
'It's a healthy sign that I've learned.'
(That's information I've not heard.)
Have some water, take just a bit,
Swill it round and take a spit
Have a tissue, it won't spread.'

The red bristle brush is the one to use
With blue and pink ones don't confuse,
Throw away the 'flossing thread'.
It's all done, now there's a charge,
38 quid, that's not too large.
It's half the dentist's bill!' she said.

Hair and Beauty

As one gets older, inevitably grey hairs appear.

The dilemma is then whether to colour one's hair or let it take its natural course through salt and pepper colours to finally snow white.

My hairdresser has an opinion on this of course, and simply asks the question: 'Why go grey when there are so many colours in the world?'

I think that is a very good question.

To Dye or Not to Dye

She looked in the mirror, and let out a scream!
Was it reality or just a bad dream?
Looking again, she was not mistaken.
Grey and white hairs a firm hold had taken.
With her tweezers she plucked and she twisted;
There were far too many, and how they resisted!

Covering her head with her new straw hat,
She fled from the house, tripping over the cat,
Jumped into the car, and in top gear drove
To the nearest shop located in Hove.
Scanning the shelves with basket in hand,
Past brushes and combs, and bright Alice bands,
She came to a row of hair-colouring dyes;
What a variety of products confronted her eyes!

Considering the tints of bright shocking pink,
But they were rejected (what would people think?!)
Or what about this—a much subtler hue?
She fancied some streaks in a pale shade of blue.
From blonde to brunette, from fair through to black,
She finally made her choice from the rack.

'Two for the cost of one', a true bargain price
She set off for home for her friend's good advice
'I'll do it for you', her pal there declared.
Gathering towels and flannels the bathroom prepared.
Then donning the gloves, and seizing the bottle,
With towel round her shoulders, trying not to throttle
Her friend with grey hair and most dismal eyes
Said, 'don't worry a bit. You'll get a surprise.'

Thinking the worst; her fear not abated,
For twenty long minutes, she then sat and waited.
Would her hair all fall out, or turn out green?
'Or orange perhaps?' She could never be seen
In public again. Of that she was sure.
With head in hands, she stared at the floor.

'Times up' the dye washed out, and conditioner applied,
'Look in the mirror', and there she espied
The grey hair gone, right down to the roots;
Her spirits were lifted, and rose from her boots.
Although the wrinkles remained, youth was restored;
She looked twenty years younger; her spirit—it soared.
'Thank you, thank you, my friend!' she exclaimed with delight.
'I can now look in the mirror without taking fright!'

Facing Up

One day, I was feeling tired and weary, fed up, and generally miserable. I decided to *take action* and get a makeover, at least of my hair.

I rang three hairdressers, all of whom were fully booked. Well, what else did I expect on Friday at 3.00 p.m.?

Usually I'm lucky when I ring the hairdresser. I have to be in the mood for small talk and was usually getting fed up with my hair falling in my eyes. I often try to trim the front myself, which sometimes works.

I decided I would try a facial at the local beauty parlour in the next village. This establishment had been recommended by a friend, and although it is a very long time since I visited one, I decided to make the effort and go.

I rang the number and was offered an appointment at three thirty. It was now 2.30 p.m., so I set off immediately and enjoyed a pot of Earl Grey tea at the little village cafe, before braving the beauty salon.

I have never been for a facial before, but have tried face masks, when people have given me them as presents. I don't usually bother about makeup because I have a ruddy complexion, and a sun tan that lasts most of the winter.

So I didn't really have great expectations for the outcome. Also the crow's feet and scraggy neck are rapidly increasing as a permanent feature of my face.

Coming out of the tea shop, I realised I wasn't sure where the beauty salon was, or what it was called, even though I have lived here for nearly twenty years. So I walked up and down the High Street looking for it. There was one at the end of the street, which I didn't know existed, so I walked back along the pavement looking for another one.

En route, I passed the ironmongers, and remembered we needed some firelighters; so I popped into buy some. I was served by a very jovial shop assistant who offered to put them in a bag, but I declined, and he said, 'Are you sure? They smell quite strong'. I said, 'It's OK they will blend with my perfume,' and we both laughed as I left the shop.

Walking down the street I remember that I was going to the beauty salon with a packet of firelighters. So I went back to the car before resuming my search. As I came out of the car park, I spotted a small shop with the sign 'THE BEAUTY ROOM', and somehow that sounded familiar 'Ah, that's better, looks a bit more friendly,' I said to myself, and as I approached the door, a bell sounded as I stepped on the doormat announcing my arrival.

There was no one in reception; only a distant sound of someone vacuuming upstairs. *'Help!'* I nearly turned and ran out of the shop!

An elderly lady then appeared at the back of the shop and greeted me by name. No escape! This assistant had more wrinkles than me, and I seriously wondered about the wisdom of this visit.

As I sat in reception and waited, reading the prices of all the wonderful treatments on offer, I wondered why there are any ugly faces in the world. If only half the treatments worked what a difference it would make!

The telephone started ringing and a second older woman came from the back of the shop to answer it. This turned out to be the beauty therapist. She was soft spoken, very kind, and informed me that J was preparing the room upstairs.

('For what? I'm only here for a facial. Why does the room need hoovering for so long? Who was the last customer, and what happened to them?)

I was beginning to be very apprehensive.

Eventually, I followed my therapist upstairs, and there a darkened room awaited with a couch. (It began to feel more like a visit to a psychiatrist.)

The therapist explained that the facial starts with a back massage.

'What? How does that work?'

But I was too scared to ask. I was left to half undress and climb, (literally), onto the high couch, to discover it was one of those with a hole for your head at one end. I was not sure whether this was to rest your head on or put your face through and await possible execution! I was relieved to see there was a towel by this hole, and promptly stuffed it neatly in.

I covered the rest of me with a blanket, and had a sudden longing for a teddy bear to cuddle for comfort. I just had to imagine though because there wasn't one.

My therapist returned and put some soft music on, so I felt a little more relaxed and enjoyed the gentle back massage.

She chatted to me about all sorts of facials and allergies, and all that sort of stuff. Well, as far as I know I am not allergic to much; I have a hide like a rhinoceros and very little gets through. I am only allergic to penicillin, which makes me ill, and brings me out in a rash. Since no pills are offered, I wasn't too anxious about that.

(*Ding Dong Avon calling; l remembered that once I had a bath in stuff called 'skin so soft,' and within five minutes had a rash from the waist down! Agony!*)

Today I decided to take a risk on the proffered treatment. After all no one else has ever reacted to it, so why should I?

It was apparently a new treatment, so I asked what was in it. The reply was vague. The only hint of reassurance was that it contained natural products. OK . . . but that could include plants and any part of any animal's anatomy, so I didn't think any further along those lines; after all it might work.

The therapist spread what felt like butter all over my face, and then put gauze on top so that I could hardly breathe. I didn't say anything, and she got the message (maybe I started to turn blue or something because she cut a small hole for my nose.

Then she smeared another layer of something on top of that and said she will leave me for fifteen minutes.

I dared not to move because the outer layer of stuff set, and I began to feel like one of the dummies in Madame Tussaud's waxworks.

Fifteen minutes is a very long time when you are flat on your back with your head halfway down a hole. I tried to relax, and practiced breathing exercises slowly and carefully. I tried to listen to the soothing music, but I was in danger of drifting off to sleep and possibly falling off the couch.

My nose began to itch, but I couldn't scratch it because that would have meant disturbing the gauze, and the setting potion! I wouldn't want permanent wrinkles in all the wrong places.

So I gently screwed up my nose, and that helped a bit, but then my eyebrows started to itch, and I needed to scratch them.

I thought, 'What shall I doooo? Perhaps I am the first person to be allergic to this stuff.'

I tried to think of something else and concentrated on the gauze; it was only cotton, and a bit like a shroud.

Quel horreur! Imagine it might be thrown away, and years later be dug up with my face print on it, bit like the Turin shroud. I rapidly changed my thinking again.

Then I had an overwhelming desire to sneeze and had visions of the gauze floating across the room, and landing sticky side up in a load of cotton wool balls, and me trying to retrieve it, and replace it on my muzzle as though nothing had happened.

I wrinkled my nose, sniffed hard, and that seemed to do the trick.

My back was stiff, and I was glad I had a massage to start with—I could understand why. There was worse to come! Some of the potion trickled down into my eye and stung like crazy. I still did not disturb the mask. I thought my facial features would be changed forever.

Just as I was thinking of escaping quietly, and creeping downstairs, mask and all, my therapist returned.

'Was I OK?' Weakly I said, 'Yes, thank you.' I hoped my ordeal would soon be over. It was! It was time for the shroud to come off, and the potions and lotions to be removed. Phew, what a relief! I was then brave enough to say about the stinging in my eye, and she washed it several times with saline.

I was then left with a glass of water, and the instruction to take my time getting off the couch. Take my time! As soon as the door was closed, I fell off the couch and reached for my clothes. I dressed rapidly. I thought it only polite to drink the glass of water, which I wish would turn miraculously into a gin and tonic.

I ventured across the room to look in the mirror and was relieved to see I looked pretty much the same—a bit more colour, and my skin felt soft as a baby's bum (which was a great improvement on rhinoceros hide).

I walked downstairs said how much better I felt, and paid a fortune for the experience!

I think I'll chill out a different way next time.

I wouldn't recommend the experience to anyone, except as an activity for 'I'm a celebrity get me out of here' or an exercise in extreme self-control for personal development.

That's Life
Cycling to Work

I've a new job in Brighton,
And need to get there by train,
But I have to get to the station,
In the fog, the sunshine or rain.

My bicycle's new and shiny,
I've oiled the wheels and the chain,
Adjusted the saddle and handlebars
And practised riding along the lane.

My helmet is blue and yellow,
With a strap fitting under the chin.
My rucksack is ready beside me,
I think I've put everything in.

Cycle clips secure my trousers,
And I've tucked them into my socks,
So they can't get caught on the pedals,
In the wheels, or in the brake blocks.

I've a spanner in my pocket,
So the bike can be folded in two,
And fit neatly into the carriage,
In the space right next to the loo.

I've already bought my ticket,
To save time having to queue,
When a voice comes over the tannoy

To say that the train is due,
and
'Passengers are reminded of that cycles
are not allowed on trains between 7.00 a.m. and 10.00 a.m.'
Oh no! Whatever shall I do?
I can't take my bike on this train,
After all the preparing I've done.
My new job's waiting in Brighton,
But I won't get there until one.
What a dilemma!
What a fuss!
I'll just have to travel on the very next bus.

Travelling by Train with a Suitcase

Been thro' baggage and collected my cases,
Tripped over my shoes so tied up the laces,
Down to the platform to catch the next train,
Holding an umbrella to keep out of the rain.
No seats in the carriage, I sit at the back.
No room for the luggage in the overhead rack,
My case has to stand on its end on the floor,
And unfortunately blocks the train's closing door,
So I alight once again,
With my case in the rain,
And vow never again
To travel by train.
(Well, at least not with a case from the airport!)

Halloween

The ghouls and the ghosties are stirring their brew,
Adding potions and lotions to black pots of stew.
They're all getting ready without being seen
For that night in October, that's called Halloween.
When witches they say, fly on broomsticks of twigs,
With pointed hats perching on flowing black wigs.
And cloaks wrapped around to protect from the cold,
It's the night of the year when they all can be bold,
Casting their spells for good or for ill,
On folks far and near to change them at will.
To princes or frogs, just for a thrill.
The black cat sits watching; it shines in the dark.
With green-slitted eyes, observing each lark.
Fairies dance freely, and goblins abound,
And elves with green tunics who live under the ground.
All are gathering together for this one special night,
When magic is practised, and many take fright
The wizards are coming muttering peculiar words,
To everyone else it sounds really absurd.
So pull down the shutters and turn out the lights,
And hide under the covers from these peculiar sights,
Safe in your bed and sleep until day,
When all the weird creatures have gone on their way.

World Cup 2010

There was such hope, optimism, excitement, and expectation this year as the England team flew to Africa to take part in the World Cup competition. I bought a flag from the local newsagent to show my support and attached it to the window of my car. Then bought a second one and displayed it on the wheelbarrow at the front gate for all to see.

My patriotism knew no bounds, and like many fans I was proud of the England team much to the surprise of my friends and family.

Football

You've got to be quick, and head it, or kick the ball to the back of the goal.
No room for fumbles, or unnecessary tumbles if you're to score, and not
    let it roll
Right off the pitch and into the ditch. 'It's a corner!' the referee's call.
The backs are in place and it's a desperate race to try to control the ball.
The crowd is elated as a player's berated for a foul on the opposite side.
There's a sense of dread at a card of red, and a sinking feeling of pride
As the team's defender, the culpable offender is sent off to the bench to
    chill out
This player's a sinner, and no way a winner, of that there's no question of
    doubt.
Into the fray flies the ball on its way, where players all anxiously wait
With heads at the ready, and legs strong and steady, to obtain the aerial bait.
With dodging and dashing, and very much clashing, the goalie grabs it
    safely away
Who with a loud crow, and a very long throw, sends it back into play.
So the game continues with stretching of sinews, as up and down the pitch
    it goes
With very much sweating, there's an end to the betting, as the final long
    whistles blows.

The match has been lost; there will be a great cost; bookies rub their hands
   in glee.
The manager's sacked; there's something he lacked; and cannot claim a big
   fee.
With heads duly bowed, their spirits are cowed, and everyone feels so down.
No welcoming fuss, no tour on the bus as they slip quietly back into town.
I'll be rather brief; it's a welcome relief to turn the telly back on.
Normal service resumed no longer consumed by football; it's finally gone!

To be honest, I found the games boring for the most part and the
commentaries annoying, so I soon reverted to watching just the last ten
minutes of each game. This beyond doubt was the best part, and it was
difficult not to be drawn into the enthusiasm of the crowds at the match
even from the comfort of one's armchair.

   We lost, inevitably perhaps, because the selection panel in their
wisdom scrabbled together the best players from across the nation. Each
man was an excellent footballer, but played little together as a team prior
to the tournament. Indeed the players had often been archrivals in the past
season; it must have been difficult to pull together, and be best buddies on
the same side, even with the best manager in the world. But then hey, what
do I know?

Just for Fun
Limericks

These rhyming verses are always amusing. I was reminded of them just recently while travelling in the underground in London. There were several examples of limericks by Edward Lear on the sides of the tube train. They are easy to make up about, just about anything and anybody. Here are my latest efforts:

There was a young farmer from Poole,
Who milked his cows on a three-legged stool.
It was quite a feat,
To pull on each teat,
And squirt 'til his bucket was full.

A flighty young girl from France,
Tried to attract all the boys with a dance,
But for all her twirling,
Leaping and whirling,
No lad gave a second glance.

Unexpected Encounter

I wandered out today,
Undecided what to do,
When suddenly round a corner,
I bumped into you,
That made my day.

My hope is that you have enjoyed laughing at life with me and enjoyed this unexpected encounter.

Index of Titles

Index of First Lines

Other books by this author: Capital letters ISBN978-1-907040

Capital Letters is a rich observation of life unfolded in a series of letters to a friend over a three year period using the authors different modes of transport(often unpredictable and unreliable) to disparate destinations.

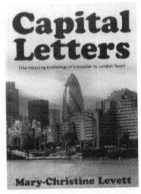

The book includes witty observations of the many people encountered by chance or by appointment as seen through the eyes of this fun loving traveller. Reflections of previous visits to the capital together with narratives of some famous places take the reader on a voyage of discovery into behind the scenes of historical events.

Reminiscences of other train journeys both at home and abroad are recorded in comic vers and prose reflecting the enjoyment and excitement of rail travel as well as the frustrations and difficulties which characterise it.

Anecdotes about tangling with ticket machines; accessing toilets, and the need for coffee and snacks occur throughout, but these are never jaded but met head on with determination and an ability to laugh at them. The letters are brought to a conclusion by the prospect of further exciting and stimulating adventures travelling and exploring London